# CAMBRIDGE LIBRARY COLLECTION

*Books of enduring scholarly value*

## Archaeology

The discovery of material remains from the recent or the ancient past has always been a source of fascination, but the development of archaeology as an academic discipline which interpreted such finds is relatively recent. It was the work of Winckelmann at Pompeii in the 1760s which first revealed the potential of systematic excavation to scholars and the wider public. Pioneering figures of the nineteenth century such as Schliemann, Layard and Petrie transformed archaeology from a search for ancient artifacts, by means as crude as using gunpowder to break into a tomb, to a science which drew from a wide range of disciplines - ancient languages and literature, geology, chemistry, social history - to increase our understanding of human life and society in the remote past.

## Pella

Gottlieb Schumacher (1857–1925) was an American-born German civil engineer, architect and archaeologist who was influential in the early archaeological explorations of Palestine. His parents were members of the Temple Association, a Protestant group who emigrated to Haifa in 1869. After studying engineering in Stuttgart between 1876 and 1881, Schumacher returned to Haifa and soon assumed a leading role in surveying and construction in the region. This volume contains the results of the first detailed survey of the ancient city of Pella, conducted by Schumacher for the Palestine Exploration Fund, and published by the Fund in 1888. During the Roman era Pella was one of the cities of the Decapolis, a group of Hellenistic cities which were centres of Greek and Roman culture. Schumacher describes the site of Pella, its extant structures and its surrounding ruins as they appeared at the time of publication.

Cambridge University Press has long been a pioneer in the reissuing of out-of-print titles from its own backlist, producing digital reprints of books that are still sought after by scholars and students but could not be reprinted economically using traditional technology. The Cambridge Library Collection extends this activity to a wider range of books which are still of importance to researchers and professionals, either for the source material they contain, or as landmarks in the history of their academic discipline.

Drawing from the world-renowned collections in the Cambridge University Library, and guided by the advice of experts in each subject area, Cambridge University Press is using state-of-the-art scanning machines in its own Printing House to capture the content of each book selected for inclusion. The files are processed to give a consistently clear, crisp image, and the books finished to the high quality standard for which the Press is recognised around the world. The latest print-on-demand technology ensures that the books will remain available indefinitely, and that orders for single or multiple copies can quickly be supplied.

The Cambridge Library Collection will bring back to life books of enduring scholarly value (including out-of-copyright works originally issued by other publishers) across a wide range of disciplines in the humanities and social sciences and in science and technology.

# Pella

GOTTLIEB SCHUMACHER

CAMBRIDGE
UNIVERSITY PRESS

CAMBRIDGE UNIVERSITY PRESS

Cambridge, New York, Melbourne, Madrid, Cape Town, Singapore,
São Paolo, Delhi, Dubai, Tokyo

Published in the United States of America by Cambridge University Press, New York

www.cambridge.org
Information on this title: www.cambridge.org/9781108017589

© in this compilation Cambridge University Press 2010

This edition first published 1888
This digitally printed version 2010

ISBN 978-1-108-01758-9 Paperback

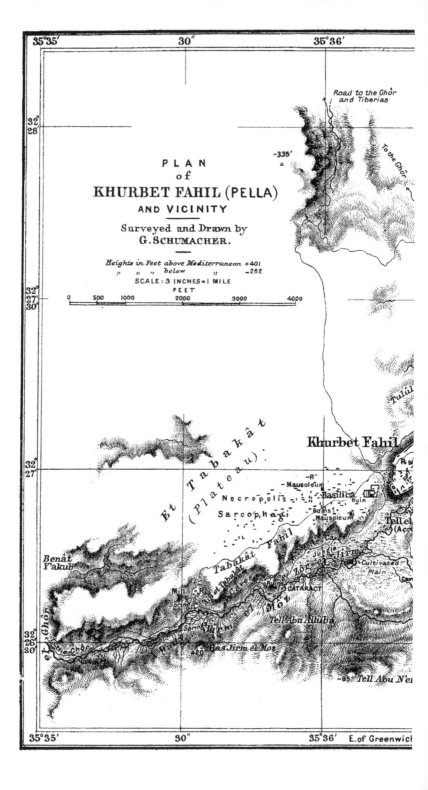

PLAN
of
KHURBET FAHIL (PELLA)
AND VICINITY

Surveyed and Drawn by
G. SCHUMACHER.

Heights in Feet above Mediterranean +401
  "     "    "    below      "      −262
SCALE : 3 INCHES = 1 MILE
FEET
0    500   1000    2000    3000    4000

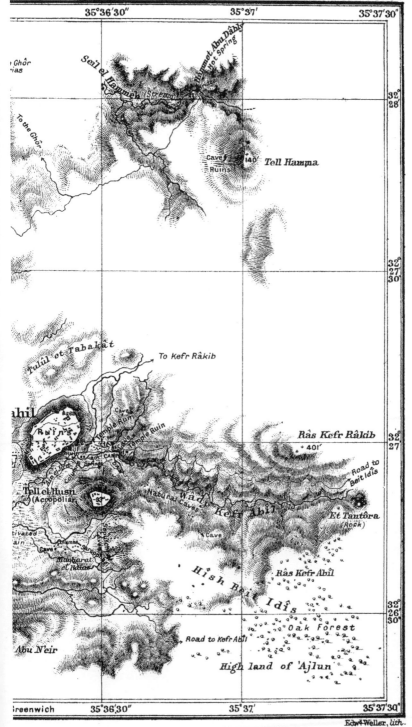

# PALESTINE EXPLORATION FUND.

# PELLA.

BY

## GOTTLIEB SCHUMACHER, C.E.

LONDON :
THE SOCIETY'S OFFICE, I, ADAM STREET, ADELPHI, W.C.;
R. BENTLEY & SON, 8, NEW BURLINGTON STREET.

1888.

# PREFACE.

———◆———

THIS work is the Survey of Fahîl (the ancient Pella), executed by Herr Schumacher for the Committee of the Palestine Exploration Fund. The place had already been visited, among others, by Mr. Guy Le Strange (see *Quarterly Statement*, 1885, p. 158). It had long been desired to procure a thorough examination of this interesting place, and the Committee gladly accepted the services of Herr Schumacher, whose descriptive map and drawings are now, for the first time, published.

# LIST OF ILLUSTRATIONS.

# PELLA.

EARLY on the morning of February 18th, 1887, we rode out of the southern gate of Tiberias, taking our course along the lake shore to the hot baths and the Jordan valley. The morning was very misty, and heavy clouds foretold us that an excursion at this time of the season would make us sufficiently acquainted with the disagreeableness of a Syrian winter. Our cavalcade could be called noble, for we were accompanied by the Governor, or Kaimakam, of Tiberias, several soldiers, an officer, servants, and some German colonists to aid me in my exploration work: we were also followed by muleteers with loaded animals, carrying, besides a tent, cooking implements and the necessary provisions, and some well-mounted Bedawîn. The Governor had less the intention of taking part in my exploration than of spending a day of rest among a tribe of the Jordan

valley, the Ghôr, which, no longer burnt by the summer
heat, presented itself as a luxurious grass growth
and a blossoming wild flower field. We crossed
the Jordan at its outflow from the lake with some
difficulty, the depth rising up to six feet and more,
and the width not being less than 60 yards; and
we first had to procure a little boat for the lug-
gage, and to drag the animals behind, which were
obliged to cross the river swimming. After this
troublesome job was accomplished we went on, and
before mid-day we rested on the borders of the Yar-
muk, in sight of the cascades formed by this river,
which rushes over large basaltic blocks near the Jisr
el-Saghîr—a stone bridge built in Muhammedan
ages, which crosses the ancient Hieromax, very near
where its floods unite with those of the Jordan.
Servants with tent pushed forwards to the tribe of
the 'Arab Segûr el-Ghôr, who were encamped little
south of the Jisr el-Mejâmia', while we took a more
eastern direction, crossed the plain, and arrived at
Esh Shûni in the beginning of the afternoon. This
little village,* containing huts, stores, and graneries,
built on the ancient site of Khirbet el-Ekseir, is the
property of our Kaimakam, who added to the Fellahîn
population some Bedawîn and Greek gardeners of
Beirût, supplied them with European agricultural
implements, planted orange and lemon gardens,

---

* *See* 'Within the Decapolis,' by G. Schumacher.

watering them by a canal from the adjacent stream
of the Wâdy el-'Arab, built grinding mills, and made

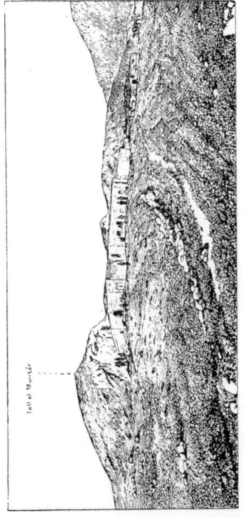

Esh-Shuni (Kh. el-Ekseir).   From a Photograph.

other improvements, which, if followed up by the
lazy Bedawîn, would soon render that part of the

Ghôr a permanently paying, flourishing garden.  We

View of Wâdy el-'Arab.   From a Photograph.

took a short refreshing swim in the above-mentioned
stream, which is bordered by oleander bushes, enjoy-

ing the picturesque view of this lower part of the
Wâdy. Here, as seen from the photograph of this
part, the Wâdy rushes into the Jordan valley, near an
old bridge, with the ruins of Abu Dabbûs, a Muhammedan burial-place, and its immediate transition
from a steep rocky ravine into an evergreen mild
valley.

It was at sundown when we reached the camp of
the 'Arab Segûr el-Ghôr, welcomed by a troop of
their best horsemen, whom we followed galloping
through this wide encampment to the place where
our tent was pitched. The head Sheikh, Raja, had
chosen for us a spot of elevated ground straight
above the Jordan river, having thus a free view over
this powerful, rapid stream, which, in endless zig-
zags, rolls southwards. The Bedawîn camping-place
was in the notable depression which bounds the
Jordan on its entire course along both shores with
steep ascents of alluvial earth, and which, doubtless,
formed the original bed of the river. We had hardly
become seated at the entrance of our tent when the
Sheikh's servants began to occupy themselves with
the preparation of a Bedawîn dinner, and therefore
spared us the conventional request for this repast
which is used among Bedawîn, in order to help the
host over the critical choice of meals. In its modest
way, it is thus uttered in the Bedawîn dialect: 'Ya
mu'az-zib, waddy Kahwa tent'alletsh (تعلّش), wa

tuthun yehatshy (يحتشي) wa dafînt (دفينة) ma
yanuttha el Kutt, wa lel Ahsân 'elbet sha'îr, wa rûh
wa ta'âl ya Muȧzzib.' Literally: 'Bring, oh host, a
coffee which pastes ;* tobacco which speaks ;† and a
heap ‡ which cannot be leaped by a cat, and an
'Elbet § of barley for the horse, and go and come, oh
host.'

We added to the frugal dinner some fish we had
caught in the Jordan, but which the Bedawîn looked
upon as 'Nijis,' or impure, a belief which I have found
now and then among the Bedawîn.

The next morning promised a fine day, and our
Sheikh would under no circumstances let us go, promising for the following night a 'Sahjy,' or dance,
as arranged on festival occasions, but generally
excluding strangers ; such a rare treat persuaded
us to stay a day longer. While the Governor
assembled around him the elders of the tribe
during the day, settling disputes and calling their
attention to Government laws, encouraging them
to cultivate soil, &c., we explored the shores of
the river and its vicinity. The female members of

---

\* That is, strong and stout.

† Good tobacco must whisper, while burning.

‡ Literally, 'dafîna' means 'the buried,' and represents a
young cooked ram covered by a heap of cooked rice, and thus
served on a large dish, forming together a meal heap 'too high
for a cat's leap.'

§ 'Elbet (علبية) means half a keil, or about a bushel and
a quarter.

the tribe occupied themselves exclusively during this
day by gathering dry shrubs and tamarisks found in
the Ghôr and in the jungles along the river, and piled
them up in heaps before our tents.

After the sun disappeared behind the mountain of
'Serîn,' bordering the western banks of the Ghôr,
and when the large flocks had entered the encampment, the dim fires gathered the inhabitants of each
tent to their meals, while now and then a monotonous
song was heard from a female member calling her
immediate neighbours together for the festival of the
evening. Soon appeared three half-grown lads, who
lighted just in front of us part of the gathered
bushes, placing arms on shoulders, they attempted
a dance with rather primitive movements, which
soon degenerated into trying to push each other
into the fire. The Sheikh's brother, a sort of Master
of Ceremonies, richly dressed, with a mighty cane
in his hand, now appeared on the tableau, drove the
boys away, and, followed by others, prepared the
field for the dance; then he uttered a long loud
cry, and groups of singing women, shouting
young men, married men and elders of the tribe
successively appeared. The latter sat in groups
around us and our tents smoking 'Ghalawîn'
(pipes) and 'Nargiles,' while a coffee, 'which pasted,'
was passed round without interruption by the Sheikh
and the 'Natûr' (a sort of landlord). The Master

of Ceremonies now set the young men one by one in a long row, shoulder to shoulder ; behind the front row a second and then a third similar followed, thus numbering altogether about 150 dancers. The young men were only clothed with their blue shirt, which they fastened in the girdle so high that their legs were bared to the knees. The fire was fed until its flames struck high over the heads of the dancers ; then the Master of Ceremonies clapped his hands, made a dancing motion, and in one moment the whole crowd of young men, with the upper part of their bodies bent forwards, clapping their hands in measure, moved towards the fire, making a step forwards and then a step backwards, shouting in a moaning, oppressed tone, 'hojîya, hojîya, hojîya.' About five minutes passed, when a finely dressed young woman, with a long blue silk robe, broke out of the rows of the women, who sat opposite the young men, at the other side of the fire, and planted herself between the fire and the dancers ; now rose the Sheikh, who, marching towards her, drew out his sword and handed it graciously to the handsome young woman—one of his wives. She received the sword, and swinging it several times around her head, danced up and down the rows of the young men, who now broke out into loud shouts and continued their dance with increased vehemence and a louder 'hojîya, hojîya.'

The young woman now put herself in a kneeling position, and feigned to be fighting with the sword with a practice and ability, which did her credit, against the crowd, which continually made rushes towards her. The higher the fire burnt the more impetuous became the motions, and the more boldly the dancers approached to the woman. Presently she sprang up from her kneeling position to her full height with a wonderful elasticity, and swinging the sword around, drove the crowd backwards. They slowly gave way, but only for a minute ; then they returned again, forming a half circle around the fighting woman and the fire. The attacks began again, and again the woman repulsed them with activity ; with astonishing changing movements the long robe and the long ends of her sleeves followed her motions ; but slower and slower became her motions until she finally fell down on her knees, hardly able to continue. This sign of exhaustion was perceived by another young woman, who stood ready behind the fire ; she ran to the fighter, who with incredible quickness threw her robe (which proved merely to be a mantle over her national costume, the shirt) over her reliever, put the sword into her hand and disappeared. The dance meanwhile was not interrupted, and the new fighter took up her duty with no less ability than her predecessor. After she also had exhausted her power, she retired ; not less exhausted were the young men, who had worked themselves into such an ardour that after stopping they fell on the ground with every sign of over-exertion.

A cup of coffee now was offered, but only a small part had the pleasure of a taste ; most of the dancers were engaged in a dispute about the dance, until the fire was lighted again, and the 'Sahjy' was renewed. Midnight was near before the piles of brush were burnt out and the physical strength of the young consumed. This dance, 'Sahjy' (not to be confounded with the 'Delky,' or ring dance, which is more common), is one of the oldest Bedawîn amusements known ; it illustrates the attempted capture of a woman ; the bravest of the young men being the lucky proprietor. Certain young men told me that a Bedawy once victoriously entered the camp of another 'Hamûl' (part of a tribe) with the object to win or rob a bride ; but their united choice fell on the jewel of the tribe, who defended her virtue with the sword, until, exhausted, she delivered herself into the hand of the most brave.

The firing of muskets and pistols gathered old and young for a moment once more ; a dance without order was tried, and then the members of the tribe left the place, singing and laughing, until the silence of the night proved that each family had retired to their hair tent.

Next morning at daybreak, while the others pre-

pared for departure, I considered with the Sheikh
and the Kaimakam the question of a reliable guide
who could serve us for our coming exploration. The
solution of this question proved not so easy, for so
lazy are the Bedawîn, especially the clever ones, that
they generally decline to engage upon the tiresome
duty of a guide, and if forced to do so, they soon
obtain their liberty again by manifesting an absolute
ignorance of the country to be explored. The Bedawy always prefers to live on (شنينة 'shnîny')
butter-milk and a piece of rough dry barley bread, to
smoke miserable tobacco, to lie on his sheepskin all
day long, rather than to expose himself to a little
physical effort for which he would be well remunerated,
and from which he could live for some time, in his
way, comfortably. Money often has little attrac-
tion for a Bedawy, but when all efforts to obtain his
assistance fail, one out of many means may yet be
tried, and that is by offering to give him sweetmeats.
'Helu' (from حلو, sweet) is the attractive word for
which the Bedawy always has an open ear; open a
sack of dried figs, of dates, of candies, or, last but
not least, of 'Halâwy' (that is, cooked sugar, or mo-
lasses, mixed with nuts), and see what a wonderful
effects it produces! Antiquities are brought to you,
parts of jewels even, anxiously hidden by a young
Bedawy woman, are offered to you for some 'Helu.'
It is the most favourite dainty the Bedawy knows,

B

and is to a wide extent taken advantage of by Jews
of Tiberias and Safed, who come bringing a small
sack of 'Kuttein' (dried figs), and return from the
Bedawîn camps loaded with bags of the best grain.
'There is an excellent guide near,' said the Sheikh,
'but unfortunately he is a renowned highwayman, and
has just been captured by a soldier.' I was anxious to
see Kasem Abu-l-Ghallûs, a name often heard in the
Jordan valley, and, promising that no harm should be
done to him, he appeared accompanied by a soldier
and a companion named Abu Ahmeïyid, also a gentle-
man of the same reputation, but who limited his trade
to the stealing of donkeys and sheep. A short examination proved that both men had a thorough
knowledge of the neighbouring country, especially of
'Tabakât Fahil,' which place was much less known
by the Bedawîn than I thought. In obedience to
the Arabic proverb, ''Ati khubzak (khaddak) lil
khabbâz, wa lau akal nusshu' (give thy bread [dough]
to the baker, if he even eat half of it), and after the
Kaimakam had promised them exemption from pun-
ishment for the crimes they had committed if they
should guide us to our satisfaction, we agreed together, and soon started, taking a southern direction, while the Kaimakan, leaving a soldier with us,
returned to his seat of government. We rode along
the Jordan valley in a blazing sun—for the Ghôr
becomes hot as soon as the sun appears—crossing the

Zôr el-Bâsha, a wide uncultivated depression, and following a path which led from camp to camp of the Bedawîn, we soon reached Tell el-Arba'în, a small hill with signs of ruins, consisting of scattered building stones. Now and then we explored the valley to the right and left, but could discover nothing else than remains of straight walls of masonry. These may have served in times past for irrigation purposes, and they are partly still used by the Bedawîn to lead the water of the Wâdy et-Taiyibeh down into the Ghôr to irrigate at the end of February those grain fields sown in the beginning of February, and which give the second crop of the Ghôr Beisân.

We were now and then stopped by inquisitive Bedawîn, of the great tribe of the 'Arab Beni Sakhr, who could not understand how Europeans should be in company with such guides as ours, but they were quickly repulsed by the proud answer of our guides, 'Mânifâdi essa'a' (I haven't got time now). A little after mid-day we arrived at the foot of the terraces, or 'Tabakât,' which form the transition from the highlands of 'Ajlûn to the Ghôr, and which from the ruin found on their southern extremity are named 'Tabakât Fahil.' These terraces form a level plateau of well cultivated soil, now and again cut through by a wâdy, and they rise to an average height of about 300 feet above the adjacent Jordan valley, or of 260 feet below the Mediterranean Sea. We climbed up the steep road, leading over limestone rocks to the mentioned plateau, and, riding for more than a mile in a south-eastern direction, finally arrived at its southern extremity, which is bordered by a precipice. Here are the ruins of Khirbet Fahil. We turned a few steps more to the east, and then went down a rough road, over *débris* and masses of fallen monuments, capitals, and columns, and arriving at the valley, camped at a place overgrown with the so-called 'Khubbeizy' grass, which here reached the luxuriant height of 3 feet. Here numerous springs gush out from the Wâdy bed, forming the lively stream of Wâdy Jirm-el-Môz. From this camping spot the explorer will receive the best idea how well hidden is the locality of the supposed site of Pella. Looking westward, to the right, we see the steep heights bordering the plateau, and the ruin we have just passed ; behind us, in the east, the course of the Wâdy is interrupted by an artificial dam ; to the left, or south, rises the mighty and steep mountain, Tell el-Husn ; while westwards extends the valley with the stream Jirm el-Môz, bordered to the north by the above mentioned plateau, and to the south, below Tell el-Husn, by a range of hills. Leaving in the eastern parts a pretty wide valley, the Wâdy soon narrows, forming a narrow ravine down to the Jordan valley. The banks are here so close to one another that neither from our camping place can any part of the Jordan valley be

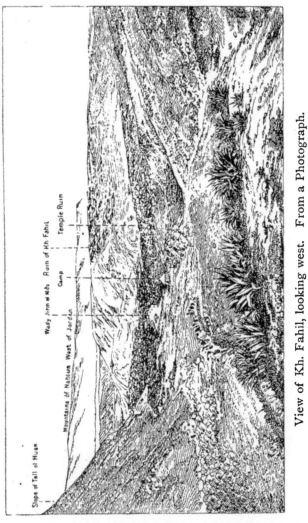

View of Kh. Fahil, looking west. From a Photograph.

seen, nor from this valley is any view of Khurbet Fahil possible—which is thus a real place of refuge. The annexed photograph shows Khurbet Fahil, with the upper part of the Wâdy Jirm el-Môz.

I now began exploring my immediate neighbour-hood, undisturbed for the present by the curious eye of a Bedawîn, for none of their camps were nearer than six miles off. A level space between the wâdy bed near our tent and the northern ascent to Khurbet Fahil is covered with gigantic remains of building materials. This terrace, but a few yards higher than the surrounding country, has a length of 50 yards and a width of 25. A long wall borders its southern part, while to the west other walls, well-masoned, partly project towards the wâdy, partly extend to the foot of the ascent of Khurbet Fahil, the north and east being protected by steep mountain ascents. This site, with its important remains, as will presently be seen, may have been that of a temple. With the aid of a crowbar, I turned over the different column heads, parts of column shafts, architraves, lintels, column bases, and hewn blocks. The building material, although of a hard limestone, rapidly becomes weather-worn. The column capitals were Corinthian, with acanthus leaves, Ionic with simple volutes and defaced ornamentation, and common Doric. The column bases are generally Attic, and several pedestals of Roman character with little projecting cornices, to some of which the column bases were worked, were found lying about; these pedestals had the form of a die (*see* sketch), each side measuring 2 feet 10½ inches. The columns were upwards of 13 feet long (that is, the combined parts of the

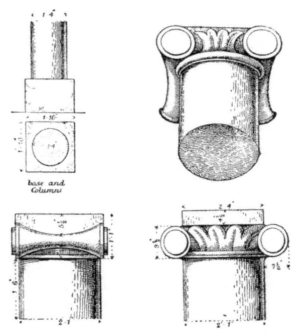

base and
Column

Ionic Capitals of the Ruined Temple.

shaft), and had a lower diameter of 21½ inches ; they were well worked, and some showed on their lower periphery the Christian emblems **A** and **W**. I also found corner columns ; that is, a couple of columns worked together, showing half of their circumference, while the other part formed a right angle ; these only have a diameter of 15½ inches. These coupled columns are similar to those found by Dr. Sepp at the Basilica of Tyre, only of a smaller size.  Of

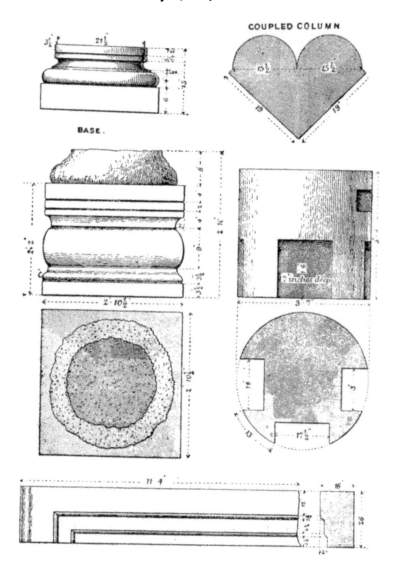

Fragments of the Temple at Pella.

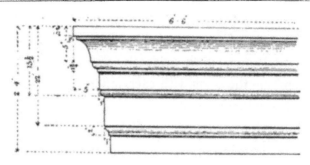

CORNICE

an entirely different character are some columns
(lying among those described) which have a diameter
of 3 feet 7 inches, and are worked in lengths (pieces)
of 3 feet 4 inches length. On some of them, which
evidently formed the base parts, we found square
holes, generally of 1 foot 4 inches wide and 7 inches
deep, and small rectangular holes above them,
5 inches wide and 3 inches deep. The first are
worked on three sides (*see* sketch), and must, as I
imagine, have been used to fit masonry work built
to them ; the small ones may have served for lifting.
These columns had evidently no capital, but merely
a small cornice. The lower part of the column was
hollowed 3 inches deep, leaving but a ring of 5 inches
width to enable a solid footing of the column.
There are also found long pieces of a top ornament,
which, as well as the lintels sketched, are carefully
carved. The lintels must have covered an opening
of at least 12 feet wide. On the upper parts of the
column, as well as the cornice-pieces, I found small

pin holes, 5 inches deep and 1¼ inch wide, fitted with a piece of iron, which was fastened to the stone with lead, and which evidently was made in order to combine the parts with each other, and to prevent a horizontal movement.

On the lower part of a broken column yet standing I found the following Greek inscription, the only one I could discover in this site. It reads as follows :—

Greek Inscription on Column.

None of the other inscriptions were legible, although Greek characters were seen here and there on the buried parts of the columns, but so entirely defaced that neither squeeze nor careful study would avail. A stone with a leaf ornament was dug out with great efforts ; it proved to be a console (corbel) with a fine volute, as seen from the sketch :—

Corbel Ornament.　From a Photograph.

Next to this stone I found another small one carefully carved, 1 foot 6 inches long and 1 foot 2 inches high, and which seemed to form part of the rib of a vault. The site is so totally destroyed that it would require considerable excavations before a good idea of its original buildings could be obtained. Besides the fragments mentioned, there is nothing more to be found at this ruin, with the exception of numerous pieces of tiles and other pottery work.

Heavy rain, which lasted with but little intervals during the whole of our stay at Pella, interrupted the exploration, and compelled us to look for a shelter in the caves, which we found for the greater part swarming with hopping creatures. The worst of this rainfall was that our tents soon became soaked, and only, thanks to the formation of the place we camped at, was it possible to keep the floods out of the interior. During the long nights we usually engaged our guides to tell us Arab stories, ' Sâlfy,' We sat around a small fire, which we kept burning in the interior of the tent, with the small coffee-can at the side of it. Ahmeîyid, a clever, lively fellow, would begin with a loud voice but in miserable language to tell the stories of the ' Beni Halâl,' the 'Ghûl' (giants), of the ' Medînet Jôhar, whence the famous jewel, ' Rîshet Jôhar,' had to be brought, and when he was embarrassed as to the continuation of the story he stirred the fire, asked for a cigarette, and brewed some new coffee. This on such occasions must be passed around, and would give him time to take up the thread of his tale again. Meanwhile, one of our party was ordered in turn to watch outside of the tent the horses, which in this wilderness were fastened to each other in a row before the tent door, with no other food but the herbage. This, however, was in no way poor, but of an abundance not met with in other

parts of the country. Our own provisions were
of little variety, they consisted in soup, rice, onions,
salad made of ''Akkûb' (عقوب) and mutton, for we
had bought a ram of a shepherd, who came near our
tent. The extremities of the animal were seized upon
with eagerness by our guides, and knowing we had
a hard day's work before us, they, as soon as
awakened in the morning, lit a fire, took the head,
feet and bones of the ram, and having cleaned the
wool but little off them, they put them into the coal,
and greedily devoured the meaty parts—although
but half done. As they could not eat up all at
once, they carefully hid what was left in a bush near,
and in the evening, when we retired to the tent again,
they looked for the remains and continued to eat, de-
claring that this was the best dinner they had had for
a long time. I often met with Bedawîn who devoured
raw meat with great appetite, or when it had been laid
but for a minute on a coal fire. One evening we were
surprised by the rapid discharge of guns, and soon after
a young wild boar was brought into our tent by a young
Arab. It had been killed by some fifteen or twenty
Christian Fellahîn, who came from the western part of
'Ajlûn to hunt in the jungles of the Wâdy Jirm el-Môz
wild boar and other game, of which the place is swarming. They do not sell the game, but after having hunted
a sufficient quantity, they return with it and unite at a
large dinner their co-religionists of their vicinity; these

festivals are generally arranged on a holiday. I invited some of their head men to dinner, among them a young schoolmaster of 'Erjân, who in the course of the evening gave me interesting information about 'Ajlûn.

As before said, the springs of Wâdy Jirm el-Môz rise just below the Temple ruin we have described ; from here downwards the wâdy is permanently fed by the springs, while upwards from the dam near the tent the wâdy bed is dry in summer. This portion of the dry wâdy is called Wâdy Kefr Abîl ; it is a steep, winding, and narrow ravine, its slopes are uncultivated, and in their upper part covered with brushwood. Along its northern slope we can follow a road which leads from the Jordan valley to the northern part of the 'Ajlûn district of Elkûra. This is much frequented, and, considering the steep slope it follows, tolerably easy to ride up. It cannot, in the absence of any distinct ancient signs, be considered as the Roman road looked for near Pella, at least not with certainty ; but in favour of its being a Roman road, I must state that from Tabakat Fahil no wâdy of the vicinity ascends so gradually as the Wâdy Kefr Abîl, and if Fahil is really Pella, this and no other road must have been the one to which Eusebius refers, and which led from here to Gerasa.

On the upper part of the southern slopes I observed

caves, but I found them to be natural and hardly ever inhabited.

The springs above-mentioned, forming the Wâdy ej-Jirm, number in all nineteen, not counting very small ones, which gush out in between. I took their temperature with the thermometer, and can state the interesting fact that I found this to be *higher* than that of the stream below, where it was no more influenced by the springs.

The following table will show their temperature, beginning with the first or most eastern spring, and numbering the others as they follow in order down the wâdy. The temperature of the air, while these readings were taken, was 60·8 Fah., which remained unchanged during the time of observations.

TABLE SHOWING THE TEMPERATURE OF THE
SPRINGS AT KH. FAHIL.

| Spring. | — | Degrees. |
|---|---|---|
| | | Fahr. |
| No. 1 | First spring, east left-hand wâdy | 77·0 |
| 2 | Below the above, good spring .... | 77·7 |
| 3 | ,, ,, .... .... ... | 75·1 |
| 4 | ,, ,, .... .... .... | 75·7 |
| 5 | ,, ,, .... .... .... | 75·7 |
| 6 | ,, ,, .... .... .... | 76·1 |
| 7 | ,, ,, powerful spring | 75·2 |
| 8 | Powerful spring .... .... .... | 75·2 |

TABLE SHOWING THE TEMPERATURE, &c.—*continued.*

| Spring. | — | Degrees. |
|---|---|---|
| | | Fahr. |
| No. 9 | Powerful spring .... .... .... | 75˙7 |
| 10 | ,, ,, .... .... .... | 75˙7 |
| 11 | ,, ,, .... .... .... | 73˙0 |
| 12 | ,, ,, .... .... .... | 75˙2 |
| 13 | ,, ,, .... .... .... | 75˙7 |
| 14 | Very powerful spring .... .... | 75˙7 |
| 15 | ,, ,, .... .... .... | 75˙7 |
| 16 | ,, ,, .... .... .... | 75˙2 |
| 17 | ,, ,, .... .... .... | 75˙2 |
| 18 | Gushes btween old masonry, powerful .... .... .... .... | 75˙2 |
| 19 | Spring called 'Ain ej-Jirm, whence the name of the wâdy; surrounded by old masonry, forming a 'Birket' and Bedawîn Bath, water power ¼-cubic metre per second .... .... .... .... | 75˙7 |

The temperature of the stream 300 yards below the last springs was found to be 68° Fah. The springs Nos. 1 to 13 discharge about ½-cubic metre per second, 14 to 18 about ¼-cubic metre per second. The springs flow into different directions over *débris* of all kinds, but finally unite somewhere in the jungle of tamarisks, canes, and reeds, called Zôr ej-Jirm. Including the small springs, they together form a rapid stream, 10 to 12 feet across, 8 to 12 inches deep, and give about 1½-cubic metre of good drinkable water per second. Having discovered that the springs are of a higher temperature than common, we soon noted what fully explains this occurrence. A little way down the stream, near what may be called the foot of the west end of Khurbet Fahil, I found the ruin of a mill, which, from its construction, must have been built in Muhammedan ages. It extends from the foot of the hill, whence evidently it was fed by a former spring, southwards towards the stream. A small water canal, 1 foot wide, 10 inches deep, is led on the top of a dyke, 50 feet long, to a round opening, and through this to the actual mill now in ruins.

This old masonry is covered on its entire length, especially on its side walls, with the deposit of hot springs, called in technical German 'Quellabsätze,' up to a thickness of 4 inches to 1 foot. The fact that I came across the very same deposit, also found on mill ruins in· the Wâdy el-'Arab,* and stated by Dr. Noetling, then my travelling companion, to be the precipitates of thermal springs, which, in the course of a relative short time, had become cool, gives us a right to conclude that also the springs of the Wâdy Jirm el-Môz were once thermal at the era of the last occupation by the Arabs, as the mill ruin mentioned is certainly not older than a few centuries. It may further be noted that the last

* Schumacher, 'The Jaulân,' pages 149–160.

C

inhabitants of Pella, Arabs, had worked this mill
with thermal waters just as the one at El-Hammeh

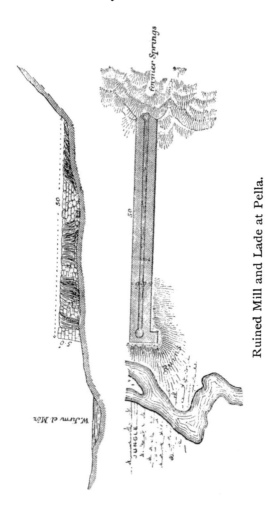

Ruined Mill and Lade at Pella.

(Jaulân),* is still worked by a hot spring up to this

* Schumacher, ' The Jaulân,' pages 149–160.

date, whence also similar proofs of the formation of such precipitates were gathered.  As such
remains of hot springs are found throughout the
wâdy, especially on its northern slopes, and as I
consider the springs observed still show a thermal
character, the passage in the Talmud of Jerusalem,*
where the city of Pella is mentioned under the name
of ' Hamtah,' or hot baths, could now be understood ;
and this, although the water was found sweet, with
the exception of springs Nos. 4 and 5 on the south
shore, which had a mineral taste so strong that coffee,
cooked from it, was not drinkable.

Near the place where the two streams from the
springs unite we find two standing columns 9 feet 5
inches apart, one of them 6 feet the other 5 feet high,
with a diameter of 2 feet 3 inches, the original object
of which could not be ascertained.  Following this
stream downwards we find on the southern slopes
numerous caves, but whether artificial or not can
no more be recognised, for the precipitates of hot
springs, which gushed out above them on the slopes,
has nearly covered their entrance, and still more
their interior, which has the most peculiar aspect of
stalactite caves.  Long, characteristic, hollow stone
pipes hang down from the roof and sides, while the

---

* According to Mr. Guy le Strange, 'Across the Jordan,'
page 273.

exterior portions shows the compact precipitates the same as those of El-Hammeh. Notwithstanding this

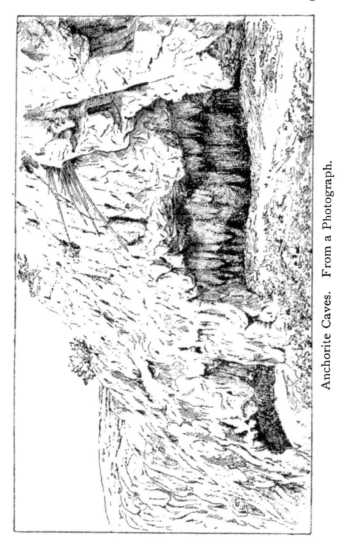

Anchorite Caves.   From a Photograph.

present altered appearance, I believe that they, as well

as their neighbours, which will presently be described,
were inhabited.

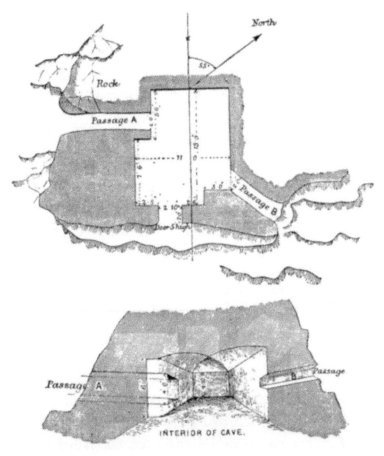

Anchorite Caves with Passages.

On a steep northern ascent I discovered one out
of the numerous caves, the interior of which, although its door was overhung with stalactites, was yet

well preserved. The above sketch illustrates the
cave, which, entering by a door of 2 feet 10 inches
wide, and yet 5 feet high, shows us a rock-cut
chamber of rectangular shape, and a ceiling cut in
the shape of a cross vault, with two pillars on the
southern and northern walls. Next to the pillars,
a little above the floor, we find a passage or small
tunnel (A) of a height of 4 feet and a width of
2 feet, which leads upwards through the limestone
rock, for a length of 10 feet, to a rock precipice in
the exterior. In the northern wall we also discover a passage (B) 2 feet 6 inches by 2 feet, which
also leads to a rock cliff, both being very difficult of
access. The cave interior and the tunnels are carefully worked. The bearing of the main axis is north,
$55^{\circ}$ west—the entire room measuring 13 feet by
11 feet. It may be accepted as beyond doubt
that we here have a cave, once inhabited by
those Christian anchorites who, in the beginning
of Christian era and during the Jewish wars, found
a refuge at Pella.[*] The flooring, consisting of earth
and remains of charcoal, as well as the plan of the
whole, has no sepulchral character, but rather that
of a habitation ; the passages being used to secure
air and escape in case of a persecution, for these
small caves, if their door entrance was carefully

* 'Eusebius, H. E.' III., 5 ; according to Robinson, ' Bibl.
Res.' VII.

shut, were hardly visible from below, and the passages still less. The entire northern slope is honey-
combed with such caves, but, to my regret, they were,
for their greater part, either not accessible or choked
by precipitates or by the crumbling rock. Below
the cave described the valley attains its maximum
width of about 300 yards, through which the river
wends its way in several branches through a thick
jungle of tamarisks, and unites again at a rocky
projection of the northern slopes, where the shape of
the wâdy suddenly assumes the character of a narrow
ravine, the stream here forming a cataract, also surrounded by thickly-grown jungles of cane, which
made an exploration impossible. Following the
stream, and turning around the precipice mentioned,
we find the upper parts of the slopes became nearly
vertical, and pierced with numerous natural and artificial caves worked in the soft limestone cliff. We
climbed over the rubbish, which was piled up in large
masses at the foot of the slopes, a product of the
rocks bordering the plateau, which crumble by the
influence of the weather, and going forwards on
hands and feet up the steep cliffs, we finally arrived at
one of the caves, which was situated 80 feet above
the stream. (*See* illustration of precipice described.)
We entered the cave, which had an entrance 5 feet
high and 5 feet wide, with no signs of masonry, then
stepped down a step 2 feet high, and followed a rock-

cut tunnel of 60 feet length running into the interior

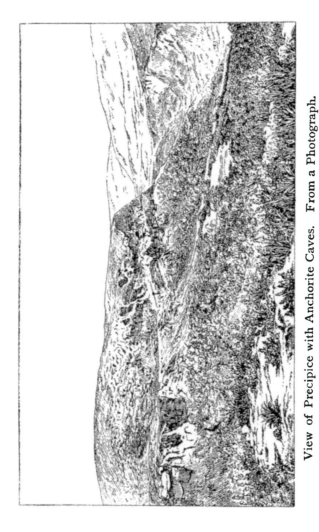

View of Precipice with Anchorite Caves.   From a Photograph.

of the mountain, until it became so narrow that
it was impossible to go any farther.  The floor

of this passage was filled up to 1 foot of thickness with manure, and the remains of countless beetles ; the roofing showed swarms of bats clinging to the bare rock, while here and there bones of animals were lying about ; the whole producing a fearful smell, which would have been unsupportable if a draught of fresh cool air had not met us coming from the interior of the mountain, which was so strong that it blew out our lights. From the entrance of the tunnel a mass of precipitates, somewhat different to those of the mill ruins, could be followed down the slope to the wâdy bed. We climbed on hands and feet along the precipice, and at distances of 20, 50, and more yards between, we arrived at a second, third, fourth, and fifth entrance of rock-cut tunnels, which could all be followed to a certain distance into the interior of the cliff, but which then became too narrow for further exploration, being filled up by mud and parts of the mountain conglomerate. In all of these a draught of fresh air could be felt. Remarkable is the fact that the bearing of these tunnels proved that they all led to a certain point in the interior of the mountain, and, as I afterwards found on the map, would nearly meet at the point where the great church described below is built on the plateau. The fact that a draught of air was felt in each of the tunnels would lead to the supposition that the tunnels joined and led to a room which was in connection with the air, and so might have been also places of refuge, or at least passages to such, in the interior of the mountain. Although I carefully searched on the plateau for a sign of entrance which might lead to such a subterranean refuge, I must add that all efforts were in vain, unless it be the church ruin, which covers such an entrance. The tunnels might have been hollowed by water streams, but then comes the question, Why were steps found in the interior of the channels, the entrance therefore *higher* than the interior? and one must observe that the tunnels rather have the appearance of being rock-hewn, though showing no masonry work. It would require special excavation work to make it possible for anybody to proceed further into the interior than we were able to go.

Taking still a western course downwards, we soon find, on the northern shore, 30 feet above the stream, another mill ruin, which was fed by a former spring on the slope. Here the formation of the rock seems an alluvial conglomerate which rapidly crumbles. While, as we have seen, the springs on the northern slopes have dried up, we see the southern slopes of the lower wâdy flourishing in an abundant growth and covered up to half of their height with jungles of 'Kusseib,' or cane; and their evergreen appearance reconciles the explorer somewhat to the barrenness and desert-like drought in which the neighbouring district is clothed at the dry time of the year. If the northern slopes were once enriched with as numerous springs as the southern ones, the Wâdy ej-Jirm must have been a much greater stream, and the quotation of Pliny (when counting up the cities of the Decapolis), where he speaks of Pella as 'abundant in water,' * can be understood. Just below the Râs Jirm el-Môz, near a round-topped hill bordering the south of the stream, but on the north shore, we find a small spring, 'Ain et-Tabakat, near which is an old subterranean vault, one yard wide, covered with precipitates, and something like a mill lade. The slopes above are also covered with precipitates of springs, which once must have been very numerous at this place.

We had, by this, nearly reached the end of the ravine, where it opens into the Ghôr, at a distance of about 1¾ miles from the first eastern spring of the wâdy. We now climbed up the northern slopes, which here are easily accessible, and, arriving at the plateau above, we found ourselves within the Necropolis of the ancient site. It is a wide field, spread with sarcophagi of common work, most of them being 7 feet 6 inches long, 2 feet 10 inches high, 3 feet 1 inch wide on the exterior. The other measurements can

---

* Plin. H. N., V., 16 (18); Robinson B. R. VII.

be seen from the annexed sketch. Their covers were fitted into the sarcophagus by a grooving, and a stone pillow was worked into the interior. A number of the sarcophagi lie in rows running from east to west, so that the pillow part came to lie in the west; but there are also specimens which lie facing other points, and with the pillow in the east. The stone material (limestone) was brought in an unfinished state to the Necropolis, and, apparently, worked out on the place of burial. I also found columns and bases worked to them of a very primitive character lying about among the sarcophagi ; some of the latter showed bosses on their outsides, as if ornaments were to be worked on them, but no such could be discovered.

There were also two mausoleums found—one of them a small rectangular building, 13 feet long from east to west, and 8 feet wide, with walls 1 foot thick, but entirely destroyed. Somewhat south, near the church, a second mausoleum of larger dimensions showed very large carefully hewn stones, and parts of a wall enclosing some sarcophagi, but although I turned over the lintel of its former square door, and other fragments, with a crowbar, I could not discover any sign or inscription.

At the eastern end of this part of the plateau, near the street which leads across the plateau down to the stream, we find the ruins of a great Christian Basilica. Irby and Mangles, who visited Fahil on

the 12th of March, 1818, write, in their 'Travels,'
while they were coming from the west, of 'the ruins
of a rectangular building, one side of it being round,
and which seemed to have been circumferenced by
columns,'* and may therefore have been the first
discoverers of this building. Guérin† speaks of a
ruin of a Christian Basilica, which he found measuring 42 paces from west to east, and 27 feet from
north to south, with three naves corresponding with
three apses, and which he believes to be 'contem-
porary with the first centuries of the Church.' He
also mentions a pavement of mosaïc.

The annexed plan will show that the above
statements are not in every way exact. Coming
from the west, we step over a strong wall, surrounding a front court of 138 feet 4 inches length and 74
feet 3 inches width, through a gate 8 feet 7 inches
wide, into the court. Stepping over scattered ruins
of columns and capitals, four of which seem still in
their original place, although fallen, and proceeding
eastward, we arrive at a sort of cross nave, or vestibule, 10 feet wide, that is to say, of the same width
as the church, and from this we enter the actual Basilica. It is of a rectangular plan, its major axis
bearing north, 95° east. Its length is 124 feet 9 inches
from the west to the concave end of the middle apse,

* Op. cit., pp. 304, 305 ; Rob., Bill. Res. VII.
† 'Descript. de la Palestine,' III part, tome I, page 290.

or 109 feet from the west to the beginning of the
apses; and 79 feet 9 inches from north to south
There are at the eastern end three apses, the two
smaller ones measuring each 14 feet 6 inches, while

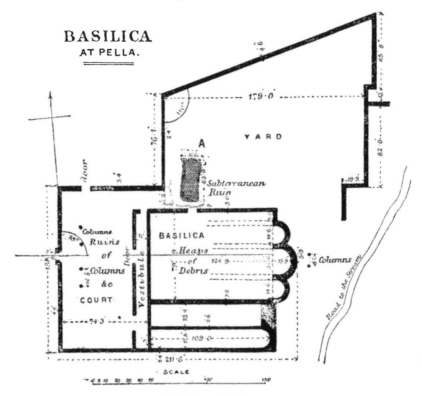

Basilica at Pella.

for the middle one and its walls 34 feet 6 inches
are left. These three apses may have once corre-
sponded with three naves, not divided by walls, but,
as usual with the early Christian churches, separated
by columns; but the heaps of *débris* piled up in

this room forbids certainty in this respect. The
northern room of 16 feet 3 inches width, which
may have been a sort of vestibule. To the south of

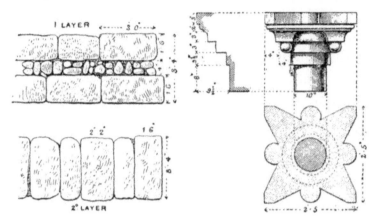

Capital and Column in the Basilica.

the Basilica there is an additional square building of
the same length, and 23 feet 4 inches width, built
on, and also south of this a second building of 17
feet 8 inches width, with an apse in the east. North of
the Basilica we find a large yard in addition to the fore-
court we have described ; this yard surrounded the
church on the north and east, but its walls are lost
where it approaches to the road. East of the middle
apse we find two columns, perhaps *in situ ;* others
lie about in disorder. The main wall generally
has a width of 4 feet 6 inches, the outline walls
have 3 feet and 3 feet 4 inches width, the separa-
tion walls 3 feet. The whole building has fallen

entirely into ruins, only the south wall of the Basilica still showing some layers built above each
other ; the wall, 3 feet 4 inches thick, shows mighty
hewn blocks, 3 feet 4 inches long, 2 feet wide,
and up to 3 feet thick, built together as sketched.
Although I could not discover any mortar between
the joints, I nevertheless judge from the construction of the first layer (*see* sketch) that a mortar
material must have been used. The columns, very
much defaced, have a diameter of 2 feet 1 inch ; the
capitals lying about were Corinthian, the bases Attic.
Some of the top cornices, which once crowned the
Basilica, showed the leaf ornament as sketched. Of
peculiar interest may also be the capitals, which
were attached to smaller columns, only of 10 inches
diameter (*see* sketch), and which have a very
uncommon form. No other details of the church are
definable, not even the doors, with the exception of
the western gate, which exactly corresponds with the
axis of the Basilica, and a northern door, leading into
the front court ; there may have also been a door in
the west of the Basilica. In the northern wall of the
Basilica we also find traces of an opening which leads
into a subterranean ruin, situate in the large yard
of the north, close by the church. We could see
nothing more than a pit, 33 feet long, 16 feet 6 inches
wide, and several feet deep, partly surrounded by
masonry. Masses of fallen fragments lie in this

depression, which must have been the entrance to some subterranean room below the Basilica, very probably a place of refuge. This room, I have little doubt, must have stood in connection with the channels just described, and it would be of great importance to carry out excavations here, which might lead to very interesting results. It should be stated that the plan of a Basilica with three naves in the middle, two to the south, and one to the north, is a composition which has no example in the early buildings of the Christian era. It is a question whether the present ruins did not form part of a Roman Basilica previous to the Christian era, which was later transformed into a Christian meeting place, or whether what we here see is not part of a crusading work added to a previous Christian church. This question which could not be solved unless the *débris* were moved away, and the disposition of the whole clearly seen, a work which, as it might bring to light most valuable facts as to the earliest Christian architecture, would give us at the same time an exact plan of an interesting monument at one of the places with which Christianity is closely connected.

The fact that *three* apses are placed here gives me the impression that the Basilica, at least the middle part, was built many centuries after the Christians fled from Jerusalem.

Leaving the Basilica we cross the street before-

D

mentioned, and at a distance of merely 100 yards we arrive at the ruined walls of Khurbet Fahil. From

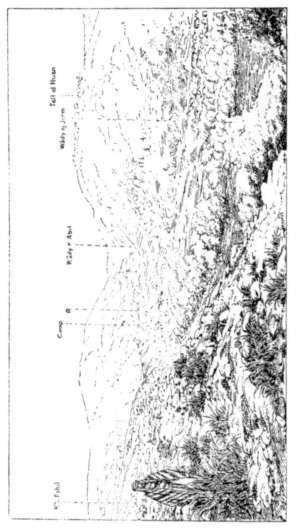

View of Wâdy and Tell el-Husn, looking East.    From a Photograph.

this point I have taken a view up the Wâdy ej-Jirm,

showing the Tell el-Husn, and the conjectural Roman road (R) leading to the 'Ajlûn highlands. As far as can be discovered, Khurbet Fahil was surrounded by a strong wall, bordering the plateau on which this ancient site is situated.

The altitude of the main part of this ruin is 262 feet (below the Mediterranean), and forms a spot which formerly must have been on a level with the remaining plateau. In the west it gradually rises 15 or 20 feet above the plain, in the north its artificial slopes are very steep and end in a valley, which partly must have been formed by throwing up these very slopes ; in the east its slopes are also steep, but of little height, while its southern part falls abruptly down into the Wâdy Jirm el-Môz. The plateau thus bordered is 300 yards from east to west, and about 170 yards across. The ruin itself consists of innumerable heaps of building stones, here and there placed together to form walls of huts, which must have been destroyed not more than a century ago, since Irby and Mangles in 1818 speak of the ruins of a rather new village,* and as also proved by the careless construction. Some of the ruins were recently rebuilt into 'Sîar,' or sheep folds, occupied by shepherds, who camp occasionally here at the evergreen pastures of the wâdy

* 'Travels,' pages 304, 305.

D 2

when the Ghôr and vicinity is parched. This recent transformation of an ancient site into modern Arab dwellings must be the cause that we cannot find any traces of ancient monuments, and but very few fragments of columns, capitals, and few cornices. The soil, however, is covered by an immense mass of hewn building stones, which accumulate in the south-eastern part of the ruin, proving that here must have stood some building of importance. Notwithstanding the absence of ornamental remains, Khurbet Fahil must have formed the actual ancient city. Strolling down its southern slopes, which have a maximum height of a few hundred feet, I discovered that they were formerly formed into terraces, each of which showed traces of a wall, which ran round the slope, numbering in all ten different walls built in regular distances from the top down to the foot of the slope. The upper wall, bordering the plateau, has a width of 4 feet 8 inches, built in layers of 1 foot 2 inches to 2 feet in height, composed of mighty hewn limestone blocks, which evidently had no mortar to combine them. This wall, which is shown in the annexed wood-cut, was built so as to leave settles of 4 inches at every third layer. The joints were vertical, but often broken.

One of the walls half way up the southern slope shows remains of arcades of a width of 2 feet 2½ inches with arches, which are horse-shoe, and there-

fore were probably erected in Muhammedan ages;
they have pillars of 1 foot 2 inches and 2 feet

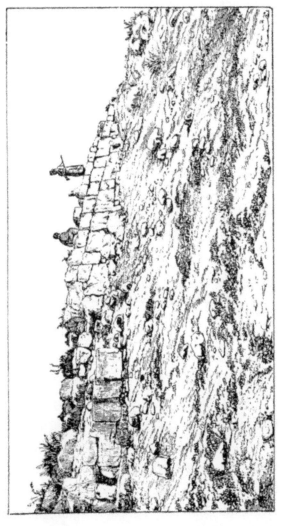

Southern Wall of Kh. Fahil. From a Photograph.

between. Only 5 feet 6 inches further up the slope

we find remains of another wall, which also shows
arcades, 3 feet 10 inches wide. The first wall is
2 feet 7 inches, the second one 2 feet thick. It
seems to me as if all of the terrace walls were

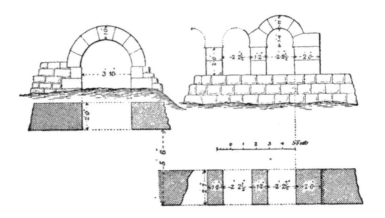

Walls with Arcades on Southern Slopes of Kh. Fahil.

built in arcades to spare building material. Now
and then a wall runs at right angles straight down
the slope, crossing the walls above-mentioned, for the
purpose of obtaining a more solid masonry.

To the north and north-east of Khurbet Fahil,
with a small valley in between, the small hills, Tulûl
et Tabakât, are scattered about, without any distinct signs of human art. Descending the slope
and arriving at our camping place again, we could
follow the line of a wall, which runs from the Temple
ruin described, along the northern slope up the wâdy.

Higher up, the slope here becoming more abrupt, are scattered ruins, masses of building stones, and fragments of columns, and now and then a cave. The caves seemed to be artificial, but the soft rock falling so quickly to decay conceals the true character. The wall of the slope ends at a sort of dam, which was built across the wâdy as if to connect the Tell el-Husn with the opposite side. The dam is well masoned, and must have supported, in ancient times, a bridge, which the winter stream of the upper part of the wâdy has totally destroyed.

Walking still beyond the bridge up the steep slopes of the wâdy, which now has the name of Wâdy Kefr Abîl, and after crossing two small side wâdies, we finally arrive high up the slope, at the ruins of a rectangular building 53 feet from east to west, and 36 feet across, the interior of which is filled with prostrate columns of 21 inches diameter, and heaps of building stones and Corinthian capitals. A large and deep cemented cistern was found aside of it. The view from this elevated point down the wâdy was a beautiful and a commanding one.

On the buttons of one of the Corinthian capitals I found a cross, carefully worked. To judge from the most careful work with which building stones, as well as the architectural remains of cornices and lintel ornaments (up to 10 feet long) sketched below, were done, together with the unusual number of finely worked columns, superior to all others which have been found on this site, it would seem likely that

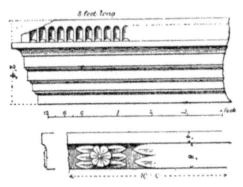

Ornament of Temple Ruin (Lintel).

this ruin must have been a temple, probably rebuilt by Crusaders. The ornament on the upper part of the cornice (Roman pipes) suggests Roman work.

Following the before-mentioned bridge, or dam, we approach the Tell el-Husn, the slopes of which show remains of walls running around the entire hill, masoned with good mortar. We follow a path leading up from the wâdy, round the eastern end of the Tell, and thus climb up its eastern slopes, which, for the purposes of attack, is the only accessible side. Having arrived at the top of the Tell, we find ourselves on a small plateau of a maximum length of 430 feet from east to west, and little less than 300 feet maximum width, surrounded by a wall of little strength, measuring 2 feet 6 inches in height, and 3 feet in width.

The plateau has an altitude of 93 feet (below the Mediterranean), or 169 feet above Khirbet Fahil, or more than 270 feet above Wâdy ej-Jirm, and is covered with scattered ruins, building stones, and traces of walls. The western culminating point is occupied by a mass of stones and strong rectangular walls, probably a fortress; several cisterns now covered up are found near its borders. The slopes of this hill are very steep, its northern and southern parts falling abruptly off into wâdies, while its western part, after an inaccessible upper cliff, gradually extends towards the Wâdy el-Jirm; its eastern slope, although bordered by a steep upper part, is connected with the high mountains by a narrow neck. Along each of its slopes we find terraces with walls built on them. The Tell el-Husn, which was hitherto not mentioned by any traveller, must have formed the naturally protected Acropolis of Fahil, or Pella. The view, down the Wâdy ej-Jirm, commanding the Tabakât, the Jordan valley, and across that over Beisân, the mountains of Nablus, Tabor, Dahy, and the mountains bordering the Sea of Galilee, as well as the scenery southwards towards the Dead Sea, is superior to any sight I have seen across the Jordan; and the position to which it owes this scenery justifies the more the acceptance of its having been an important place of foregone ages.

Eastward the view is less imposing, as the highlands of 'Ajlûn rise 1,000 and some hundred feet higher.

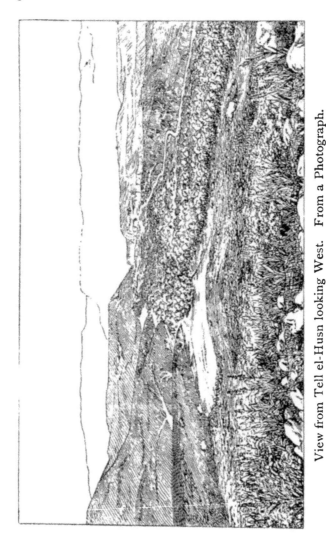

View from Tell el-Husn looking West.  From a Photograph.

We crawled on hands and feet down the southern slope

of the Tell, over terraces and walls, of which merely
the foundations were to be seen, the other masonry
having been washed down to the bottom by the rain,
and accumulated there, or carried off by the wâdy.
Half-way down the height we passed a remarkably
large rock, which projected out of the hill side, and
which was covered with precipitates of springs. The
tradition of this spot is that, long before, a princess,
Bint el-Ghatrîf (غطريف), brought the spring of Wâdy
ej-Jirm up to the plateau of Tell el-Husn, and that
this spring was afterwards led down the slope to this
rock to work a mill. Although this tale has little
credibility, it is nevertheless a fact that either the
Acropolis possessed a spring, or was supplied from a
distant one (but certainly not from the wâdy), the
water of which was led over this rock; the precipitates can be followed down the slope. At the
foot of the Tell, especially in the south-west, we
recognised scattered ruins of buildings. Crossing
a small wâdy bed, and proceeding southwards to a
little plain, we arrived at a small hill, at the northern
foot of which a column is still standing, while others
are spread about among building remains. The
mound itself is artificial, thrown up over a cave,
or several caves, called Mugharat el-Halas, حلس
the western and eastern entrances of which, as well
as other parts, are fallen in; its doors were formed by
carefully hewn stones, and shut by a stone gate. An

exploration in its present state was impossible. We proceeded eastwards, over a field covered with *débris* and sarcophagi, most of which were broken and lying about in disorder, and arrived at the hills which border the small plain. We found about a third way up the slopes a number of caves of sepulchral character. The first of these caves contained, as seen from the plan, five kokim in the northern and five kokim in the southern wall, and two loculi in the eastern wall, while near the entrance, in a sort of fore-room, three other kokim are worked in the southern wall. A widened entrance of 13 feet is cut into the rock, forming a vestibule for the actual gate, which, 4 feet 7 inches high, and 3 feet 7 inches wide, and showing no masonry, leads into the fore-room mentioned, and through a second gateway of 9 feet 4 inches in width, into the sepulchral chamber, which measures 22 feet 6 inches by 14 feet 8 inches; the whole disposition thus having the character of a cross. The kokim are each 6 feet 6 inches long, 2 feet 6 inches wide, and 2 feet 10 inches high, leaving walls 2 feet 2 inches wide between; the loculi are 8 feet 2 inches long and 6 feet 6 inches wide, and 3 feet 4 inches high with a rounded upper part. The height of the cave, from floor to ceiling, is 5 feet 11 inches; the whole is rectangular and carefully worked out of a very soft limestone rock, showing no masonry whatever. The major

axis is N.W. Cave No. 2 (*see* plan) shows an
entrance carefully bordered by hewn stones 2 feet
8 inches wide, and a stone gate (still perfect),

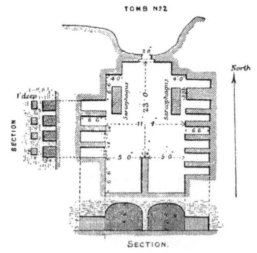

Cave or Tomb, No. 2.

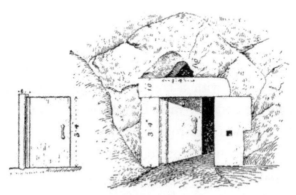

Doorway of No. 2.

which leads immediately into the sepulchral room.

Here we find, on the east, seven kokim, four on the west, and two loculi on the south, leaving a central room 23 feet by 11 feet 4 inches. The other dimensions are seen from the plan. Above the kokim we find small holes, 1 foot 8 inches by 1 foot 8 inches, and 1 foot deep, which may have served for lamps. Near the entrance two sarcophagi of basalt are placed, with covers of rough work. The major axis is N. ; the whole is rock-hewn but fallen to decay. Cave No. 3 shows us a room of 23 feet by 13 feet, with five kokim in the northern and eight in the southern and western walls, with an unfinished loculus on the east. Also here we find the holes before-mentioned above the graves, but 2 feet in height, 1 foot 6 inches in width, and 2 feet in depth. The height of the cave is 5 feet 6 inches. Its major axis shows exactly W. ; in the south-eastern corner we find a mill-stone. The entrance of this cave is widened before the door is reached, which has 2 feet 7 inches width, and which shows a fine ornamentation on its lintel, with a cornice all round (see sketch). Above the doorway there is an opening 1 foot 8 inches high, cut into the rock. To the right hand of the door, worked out of one of its bordering stones, there is apparently a small altar, 1 foot 5 inches high, with a human figure, the head of which is unfortunately broken. The top of this altar shows a circular hole, probably destined for libations to the dead. This

doorway, which is on a line with the northern wall of
the cave, shows hinge-holes of a stone gate, which has

Entrance to Tomb or Cave No. 3.

disappeared.   Next to this cave we find another, with
four small kokim on the north, and two loculi on the
south, but with no other signs of interest.   Cave No. 4
can be entered by a western flight of stairs and
a rock-hewn door of 4 feet by 2 feet 6 inches, showing
an unfinished interior of 18 feet by 12 feet, with a
sarcophagus lying on the east of the sepulchral room ;
this sarcophagus is of limestone ; its appearance is
given in the sketch.   Next to this is a cave with a

stone gate, but the entrance which has fallen in makes
an exploration impossible.   Cave No. 5 shows an en-

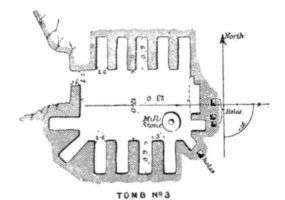

TOMB Nº 3

Tomb or Cave, No. 3.

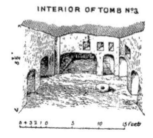

trance which is masoned with small building stones
to support the very soft and crumbling rock.   Within
a room of 25 feet by 16 feet shows six kokim on
its northern and five on its southern wall ; from here
an almost closed opening leads into an unfinished
adjacent eastern room of 20 feet by 12 feet, showing
seven unfinished kokim ; this cave seems to have been
plastered, its major axis points towards the west.   In

the roof of this cave I discovered a plate of burnt pottery, 1 foot square and 2 inches thick; after removing it from the rock, I found it to cover the part of a grave, which still contained fragments of human bones, nearly fallen to dust. I conclude that this grave is much older than the grave below, as it must have been dug before the cave was finished. No signs on the surface of the earth betrayed the existence of the burial place.

The caves found along the slopes amount in all to fifteen, all being of the character just described; most of them are temporarily occupied by herds, and the interiors of all of them, without exception, swarm with fleas so that we were only able to remain a minute while exploring, and then rush out to gain fresh air. We soon found it best to deprive ourselves of our clothes, and to continue exploration in a Paradise-like costume, by which means we got quickly rid of our enemies.

The above is all that was found in or near Khurbet Fahil. The southern vicinity of the site has little importance ; the hills, which are marked on the map, the Tell Abu N'eir, the Tell Abu Allûba, show no signs that they were ever occupied. In the Ghôr below the Tabakât there are, it is said, scattered ruins and trees, called Benât Yâkûb; but my official duty called me back to the Liva, without being able to explore them.

E

What has been described above may give us the
certainty that Tabakât Fahil, with its Khurbet, and
the Tell el-Husn, were places of very considerable
importance; but, in the absence of inscriptions, we
are not yet justified in stating without doubt that
Fahil is identical with Pella. Renowned authorities
have brought forward evidences in favour and dis-
favour of this identification. The name of Pella
is evidently lost, but that of the more ancient Butis
(Steph. Byz., Πέλλα πόλις κοίλης Συρίας ἡ Βοῦτις
λεγομένη) seems to be preserved in the present Beit
Idîs, a village on the western borders of the 'Ajlûn,
the slopes of which run down to the Tell el-Husn;
further, also, the slopes from this Tell upwards to
the east are called Hîsh Beit Idîs. In the evidence
brought together in favour of its being Pella of the
Decapolis, (among which especially that of Robinson*
must be named, who first identified this site, and that
of Guérin,†) it seems to me that the facts noted by
Guy le Strange‡ deserve attention. According to him,
Yakût, in his 'Geographical Encyclopædia,' states that
'the battle of Fihl, which took place within the year of
the capitulation of Damascus, is likewise known under
the appellation of the Day of Beisân.' This is of

---

* 'Bibl. Res.' VII.

† 'Descript. de la Palest.,' III. partie, p. 288.

‡ 'A ride through 'Ajlûn and the Belka' in 'Across the
Jordan,' p. 272, ff.

great value for this identification, for Beisân lies just
opposite Fahil, on the other side of the Ghôr ; and
thus the battle fought could be named after one of
these places as well as the other, a fact which could
not be brought into correspondence with the sites
which, proposed by others, as Eli Smith, or Seetzen,*
the latter (or at least his commentators) taking Sûf
in 'Ajlûn for Pella.

Besides Fahil, there is no place in the neighbour-
hood which shows such important ruins, sepulchral
and inhabited caves, abundance of water, &c., and no
name of a similar sound with Pella was discovered, if
it is not Khurbet Abu Felâh (فلاح), a small ruin
mentioned to me, which lies in the interior of 'Ajlûn,
and which I hope to visit soon.

We left Khirbet Fahil while blessed with a heavy
rain, and hearing that near a certain Tell Hamma,
which was pointed out to me from the top of Tell
el-Husn, a hot spring was to be found, I proceeded
northwards and turned into the deep ravine, which
runs north of the Tabakât into the Ghôr. The road
up this wâdy—if it can be called a road—leads along
slippery slopes, which in their upper part are bordered
by high perpendicular crumbling rocks, and which
near the little stream show a formation of gray clay,
down which our horses continually slipped. After

---

* 'Reisen durch Palâstina, &c.,' (Kruse), vol. IV., p. 198, ff.

riding about a mile up the wâdy the road became
no more possible, we therefore forded the stream
called Seil el-Hammeh, and, picking our way
through jungles of cane and brush, we finally
arrived at the hot spring called Hammet Abu
Dâbly. This thermal spring gushes out of the
wâdy bed, forming a small natural basin, from
which a little stream of ½-cubic foot per second
flows off; the water is sulphurous, but drinkable
like that of Hammeh, near Umm Keis. I found its
temperature to be 104° Fah., at a temperature of
the air of 68°.

The bushes which surround the basin are covered
with bits of rags of all colours, offerings by women,
who, in hope of children, use this bath, to which they
attribute help, as well as to that of the Northern
Hammeh. The ravine from this spring eastwards
suddenly widens, forming a lovely valley. To the
north of Hammeh, close to the spring, we find the
ruins of a small rectangular building, which, to judge
from its mighty, carefully hewn blocks, is of Roman
origin; these blocks measure up to 4 feet length by
2 feet height and 2 feet width. This ruin seems
rather too small for a bath, but may have been a
watch-tower to protect the thermal spring. The whole
vicinity is pervaded by a strong sulphurous smell;
and 80 yards further up we arrive at a second small
spring, which, nearly dried up, is also of thermal

character. Many others of less importance lie along the wâdy bed.* Over the second spring a natural bridge, hewn out of the soft limestone rock, spans across the wâdy, which from here upwards has no water in summer. This bridge is cut through the rock in a length of 28 paces, it has a width of 14 paces, and the arch is 10 feet to 14 feet high. The annexed sketch will illustrate the grandeur of the appearance of this mighty rock, and its passage below, which in ancient times must have been widened by human art to its present state. We rode up a path north of this bridge, which, by several windings, brought us up to the top of the rock plateau. We heard that this bridge forms a welcome passage in winter, when the deep wâdy otherwise would be nearly unfordable. We proceeded on the path chosen, south-eastwards up to Tell Hamma, close by, which I found to be a hill of a regular shape, with a plateau on its top, attaining to an altitude of 140 feet above the Mediterranean. I had no time to explore the Tell more thoroughly, and can only state the presence of scattered ruins, artificial slopes, and some caves.

On our way back to the Ghôr we no longer followed the wâdy bed, but found a more practicable road above its southern borders, along which path

* I also discovered precipitates of hot springs.

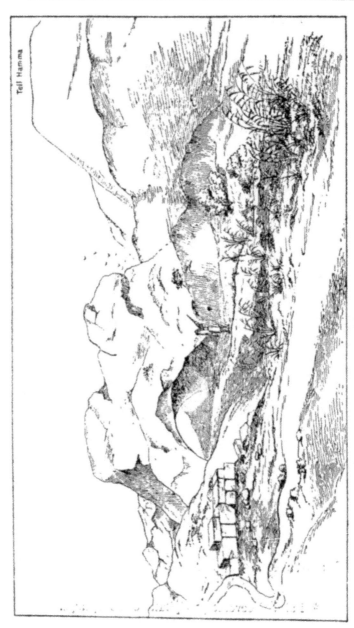

Tell Hamma

View of natural Rock Bridge.   From a pencil sketch.

we had a fine view down the ravine. The picturesque formation of long stretched, steep ranges
of hills, is curiously cut into by the stream and the
rain, which leave after every winter distinct signs
of their destructive character on the crumbling white
rock.

We reached the Ghôr at the place where the Seil
Hammeh enters it, at 11.30 forenoon, and riding
northwards came, at 12.0, to a ruin called Merkà,
situated close to the Wâdy Abu Ziâd, with a lively
stream overgrown by Kusseib. The ruin, situated
on a small elevation shows nothing but scattered
building stones. The mound is surrounded by a
lovely valley, bordered on the north by the Jebel
Skeiyin, and on the south by a hill called Umm
ed-Dubâr. We proceeded 400 yards more, and then
struck a road leading up to a village called 'Arâk
Abu Rijdân. This village, which contains about
thirty huts, is situated on a high rocky mountain
top, straight above the Ghôr, and has the appearance
of a small fortress. Several springs on its slope, and
the large Wâdy es Siklâb, which carries a large
amount of water, supply the village with water.
Before crossing the lively stream of Wâdy es-Siklâb,
we passed a stony field called Ibseily, opposite which,
on the north bank of the stream, there were very
ancient ruins of a mill, and other scattered building
stones, called El Kala'ât. East of this close to the

road, there are bare, large black rocks, called Hajâr
es-Sûk, close to which, in ancient times, a market used
to be held ; 200 yards to the west rises Tell Arbâîn,
mentioned before. To the north, the Wâdy es-Siklâb,
with its fertile valley, is bordered by the rocky hill
Tell el-'Ezziyeh, on the other side of which we cross
the large Wâdy et-Taîyibeh, with its rapid powerful
stream ; and a few hundred yards beyond, the ruin
Wakkâs is reached. The remains consist of a large
mill ruin, once carefully built, to the north of which
there are forty winter huts, built of stone and mud,
the property of the village of et-Taîyibeh.* Among
the huts there is an old Muhammedan Wely of Sheikh
Wakkâs, shaded by Sidr trees. Still a few hundred
yards northwards we come to the Wâdy Mendâh (*see*
map of 'Ajlûn, Schumacher) ; then to a path leading
up the slopes to et-Taîyibeh, and a few minutes
beyond to a wâdy, which in its upper part, where it
has water, is named Wâdy el-Kusseib, while its dry
part below the road is called Wâdy el-Husa. Down
in the Jordan valley, near where the Wâdy el-Bîreh of
western Palestine joins the Jordan, there is a small
ruin and hill, called Tell Abu 'l-Kamel ; and 1,500
yards to the north of Wâdy el-Kusseib we arrive at
Tell Seirawân and Freikâ, places mentioned in my
map and account of 'Ajlûn. Near Khurbet es-Sâkhni
(*see* same map) there is a dam, evidently artificial, of

* See Schumacher, 'Within the Decapolis.'

earth projecting from the slopes, across part of the
Ghôr, which is called el-Midras (wall). I explored
Khurbet es-Sâkhni, near Ma'âd, again, and found
some caves along the Ghôr which have a sepulchral
character; but the conglomerate rock is so rapidly
falling to decay, that nothing could be planned except
a more or less irregular door, a rock-hewn interior of
10 feet by 10 feet, and some kokim.

In the earlier part of the afternoon we were able
to pitch our tent at Esh-Shûni again. Next morning
we baksheeshed our highwaymen-guides with presents
and money. I asked what they intended to do with
the money; 'Nishtery hala lil beit' ('We will buy
some sweetmeat for our home'), they replied. As I
thought that they would get too much of it if they
spent the money in this way, I enquired further, and
received the answer, 'Nishtery tshîs kuttein lil bîa'
('We will buy a sack of dried figs and sell it'). I
tried to convince them that they ought to save up
the money for a time of want, but, evidently aston-
ished, they replied, 'Ya! bidna nakhawwy nûh?'
('Alas! shall we obtain the age of Noah?')

After receiving this philosophical reply we mounted
again, and took our way back to Tiberias.

# INDEX TO THE NAMES.

Merka' مرقع, 71.

el Midras مدرس "Wall," 73.

Mugharat el Halas مغارة الهلس "The cave of the stone couch," 59.

Necropolis, 44.

Râs Jirm el Môz راس جرم الموز "The mountain head of Jirm el Môz," 43.

Râs Kefr Râkib راس كفر راكب "The mountain head of Kefr Râkib."

Râs Kefr Abîl راس كفر ابيل "The mountain head of Kefr Abîl."

Seil el Hammeh سيل الحمّة "The stream of Hammi," 68–71.

Serîn, Mountain of, 13.

Sheikh Raja, 11.

Sheikh Najas, Wely of, 72.

esh Shûni (Kh. el Ekseir) الشونة "Granary," 8, 73.

Tabakât Fahil طبقات فحل "The terraces of Fahil," 18, 20.

et Taîyibeh الطيّبة "The good," 72.

et Tantôra الطنطورة "The peak."

Tell Abu 'Allûba تلّ ابو علّوبة, 65.

Tell Abu 'l Kamel تلّ ابو القمل "Hill father of the house," 72.

Tell Abu N'eir تلّ ابو نعير "The hill of the little *N'aûrah*, a wheel for raising water," 65.

Tell el Arba'în تلّ الاربعين "Hill of the forty (Saints)," 19, 72.

Tell el 'Ezzîyeh تلّ العزّية 72.

Tell Hamma تلّ حمّة "Hill of the hot spring," 67.

Tell el Husn تلّ الحصن "Hill of the fortress," 20, 51, 56.

Tell Seirawân تلّ سيروان "Hill of cypresses ?" 72.

Temple, Ruins of a, 54, 55.

Tombs and Sarcophagi, 60.

Tulûl et Tabakât تلول الطبقات "Hills of the terraces," 54.

Umm ed Dubâr ام الدبار "Mother of wild bees," 71.

Wâdy el 'Arab, Mills in وادي العرب "The water bed of the 'Arab," 9, 33.

Wâdy Abu Ziâd وادي ابو زياد "The water bed of the aggressive," 71.

Wâdy el Bîrch, 72.

Wâdy el Husa وادي الحصى "The water bed of the pebble stone," 72

Wâdy Kefr Abîl وادي كفر ابيل "The water bed of K. Abîl," 30, 55.

Wâdy el Kusseib وادي القصيب "The water bed of the cane," 72.

Wâdy Jirm el Môz وادي جرم الموز "The water bed of the Jirm," 20, 22, 29, 30, 57.

Wâdy Mendâh وادي مندح "The water bed of the damp place," 72.

Wâdy es Siklâb وادي السقلاب "The water bed of the Slavonians," 71, 72.

Wâdy et Taîyibeh وادي الطيبة "The water bed of the good," 72.

Wakkâs وقاس 72.

Zôr el Bâsha زور الباشا "The depression of the Pasha," 19

Zôr ej Jirm زور الجرم "The depression of Jirm," 32.

THE END.

For EU product safety concerns, contact us at Calle de José Abascal, 56–1°, 28003 Madrid, Spain or eugpsr@cambridge.org.

 www.ingramcontent.com/pod-product-compliance
Ingram Content Group UK Ltd.
Pitfield, Milton Keynes, MK11 3LW, UK
UKHW012336130625
459647UK00009B/320